BOLD KIDS

North Carolina

CHILDREN'S AMERICAN LOCAL HISTORY BOOK

No part of this book may be reproduced or used in any way or form or by any means whether electronic or mechanical, this means that you cannot record or photocopy any material ideas or tips that are provided in this book.

Copyright 2022

All images in this book have been reproduced with the knowledge and prior consent of the artists concerned, and no responsibility is accepted by producer, publisher, or printer for any infringement of copyright or otherwise, arising from the contents of this publication.

The state is also home to America's first airplane. The Wright Brothers' historic flight on December 17, 1903, lasted 12 seconds and traveled 120 feet. They flew the same plane three more times before it landed and was destroyed beyond repair.

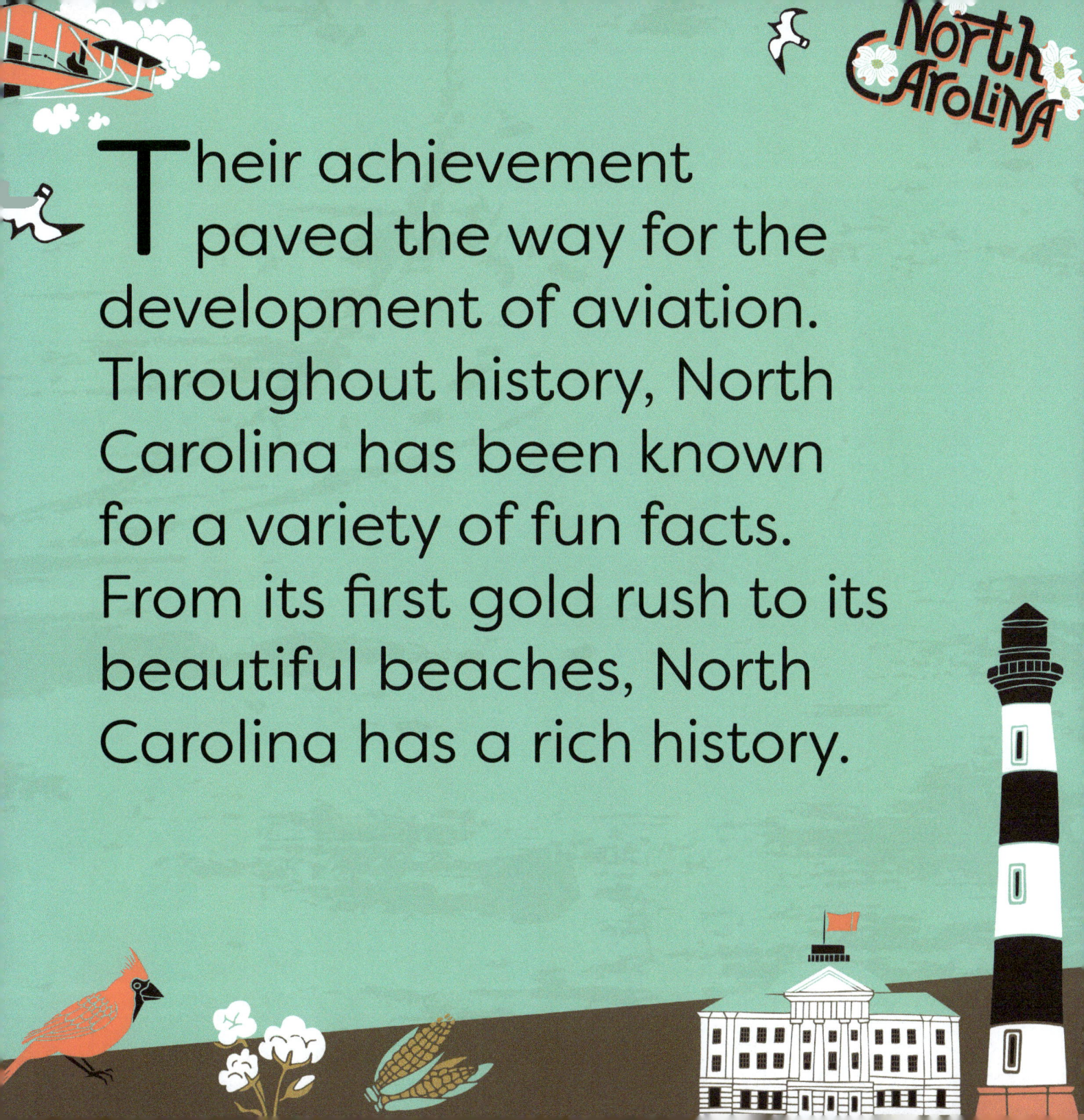

Their achievement paved the way for the development of aviation. Throughout history, North Carolina has been known for a variety of fun facts. From its first gold rush to its beautiful beaches, North Carolina has a rich history.

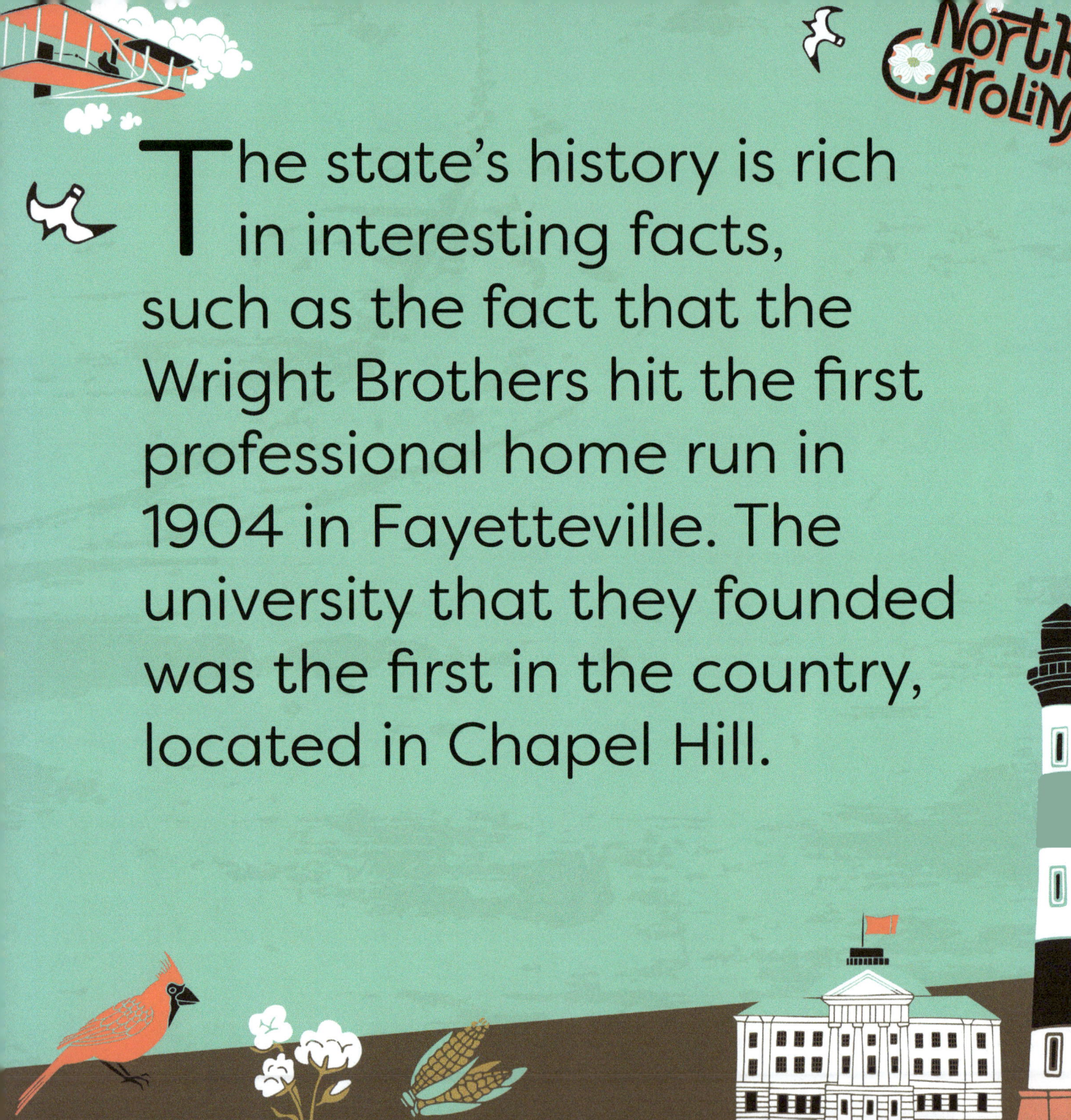

The state's history is rich in interesting facts, such as the fact that the Wright Brothers hit the first professional home run in 1904 in Fayetteville. The university that they founded was the first in the country, located in Chapel Hill.

And the Wright brothers' first sustained powered flight took place in Dare County. The state is also home to the Wright brothers. It's full of unique and fun facts that will make learning about North Carolina a fun experience for your children.

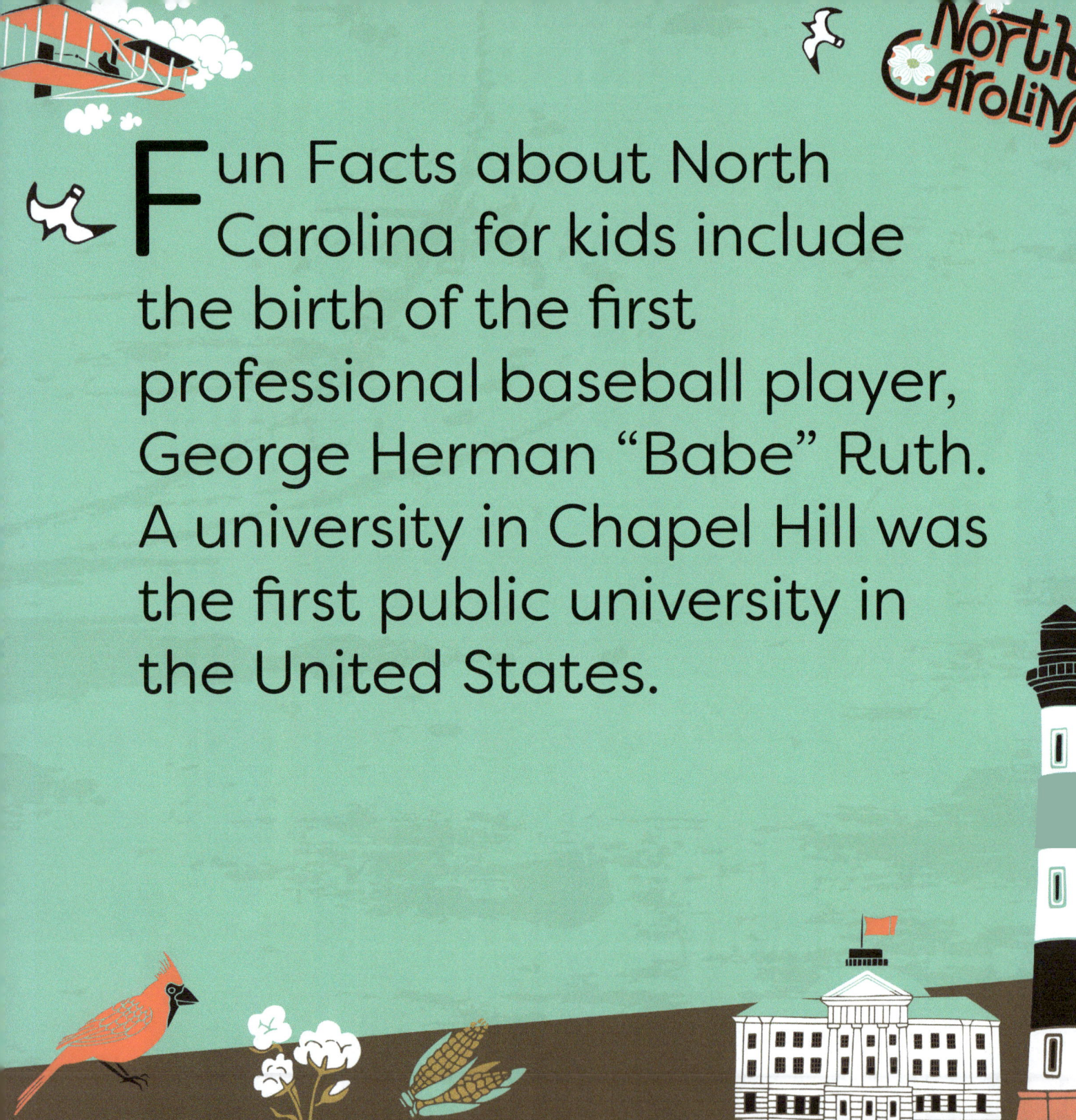

Fun Facts about North Carolina for kids include the birth of the first professional baseball player, George Herman "Babe" Ruth. A university in Chapel Hill was the first public university in the United States.

The Wright brothers also launched the world's first powered flight in the Dare County area. The state has many more interesting and unique things to offer for kids. You'll be pleasantly surprised at the fun facts about North Carolina for kids in the state.

If you're a parent who wants to educate their children about the history of their state, you can share the fun facts with your children. If your children love history, they can learn more about the Carolina Hurricanes.

They'll love the Panthers, and their first pro sports team. By teaching them about these interesting and fun facts about North Carolina, you'll be able to make them happy as well.

A fascinating and interesting fact about North Carolina for kids is that the state was the first to be admitted into the union, and the first gold rush took place here. Today, North Carolina is a thriving state with many unique and interesting facts.

The country's most famous people were born in North Carolina. In addition, the state has many other important landmarks. For example, the Wright Brothers first flight took place in the state of Northam.

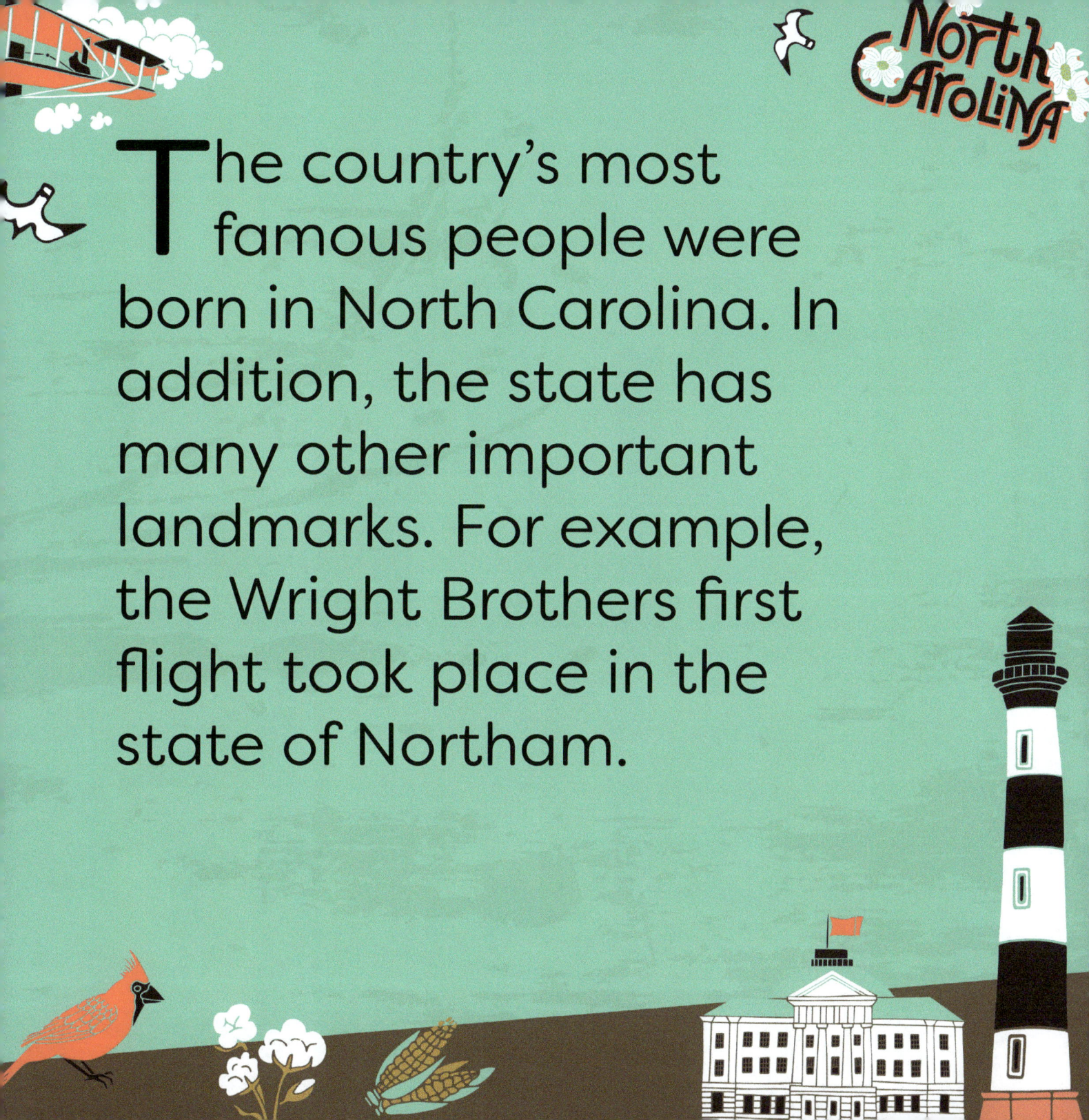

Fun facts about North Carolina can range from the state's history to its famous people. The city's oldest lighthouse, the first gold rush, and the state's first gold mine. Various historical events have also taken place in the state.

For example, there is a rich history of the Wright brothers. And, the Wright brothers are the first people to fly the world. There are many other interesting facts about North Carolina for kids in the U.S.

The state is home to a lot of famous people. Some of these were born in the state. In fact, the Carolinas are home to many famous people. For example, Andrew Jackson is the president of the United States.

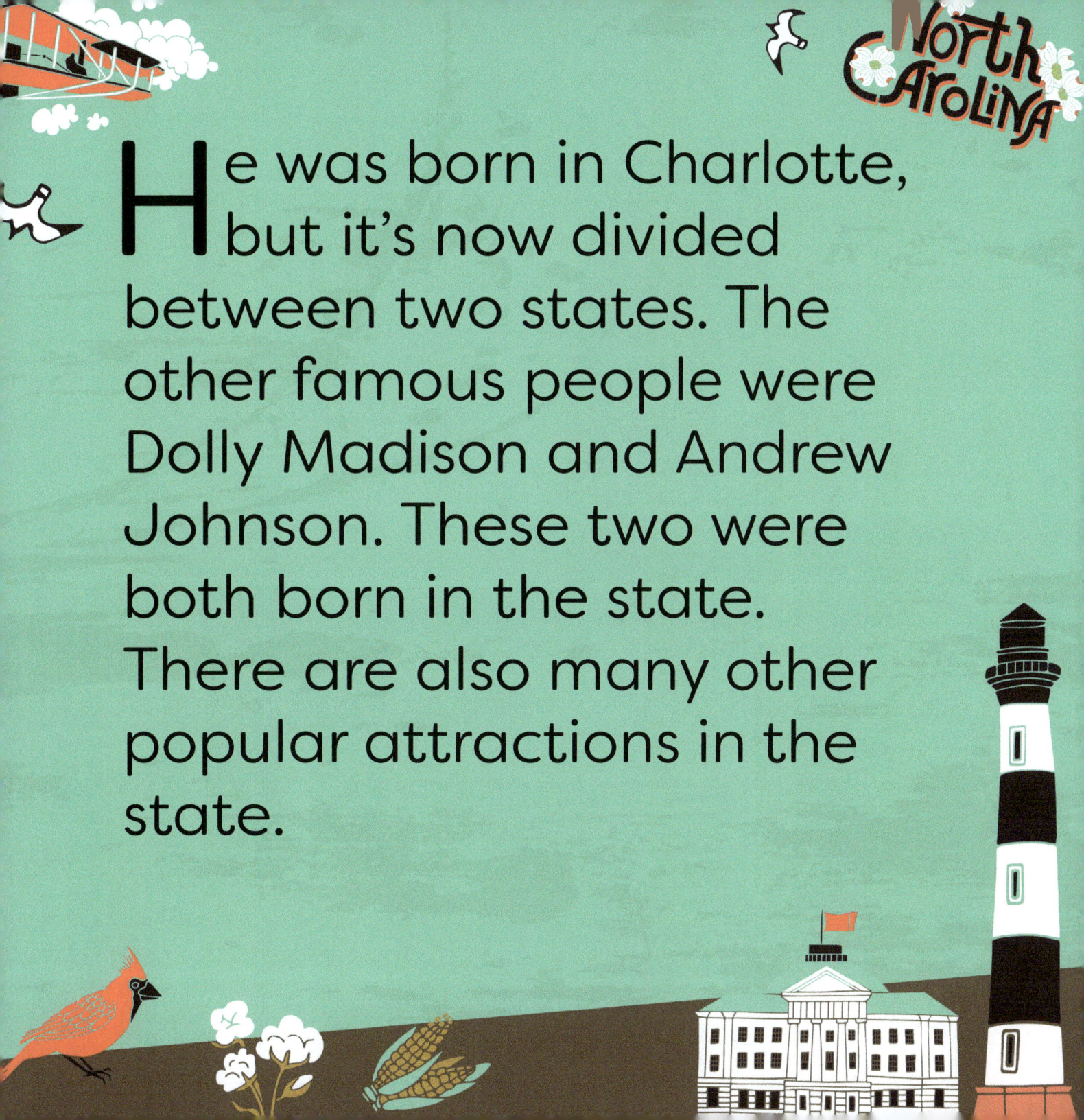

North Carolina

He was born in Charlotte, but it's now divided between two states. The other famous people were Dolly Madison and Andrew Johnson. These two were both born in the state. There are also many other popular attractions in the state.

Milton Keynes UK
Ingram Content Group UK Ltd.
UKHW051116060923
428116UK00006B/43